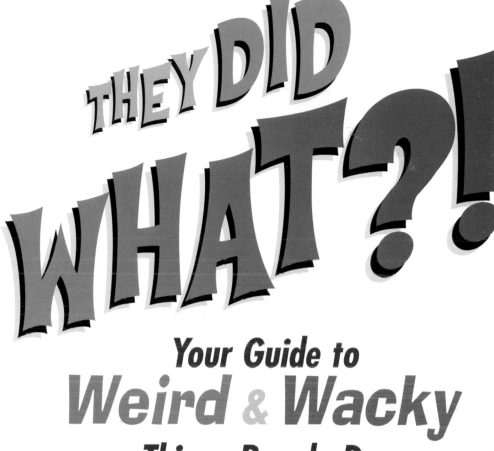

THEY DID WHAT?!

Your Guide to
Weird & Wacky
Things People Do

written by
JEFF SZPIRGLAS

illustrated by
DAVE WHAMOND

MAPLE
TREE
PRESS

Maple Tree Press Inc.
51 Front Street East, Suite 200, Toronto, Ontario M5E 1B3
www.mapletreepress.com

Distributed in Canada by Raincoast Books
9050 Shaughnessy Street, Vancouver, British Columbia V6P 6E5

Distributed in the United States by Publishers Group West
1700 Fourth Street, Berkeley, California 94710

Dedication
Dedicated to the banana peels of the world, especially the ones that got slipped on.

Acknowledgments

225 6406

A great number of people helped with the preparation of this book. Among the many, I'd like to thank the following for their help with the fact-checking of some of the information: Marc Abrahams, Tavis J. Basford, Michael Dewar, Ronald J. Leprohon, Carl Mehling, David Schmidt, Elizabeth Semmelhack, Rich Vieira, and Bill Young (webmaster of www.nywf64.com). The BURGER KING® and WHOPPER® trademarks are used with permission from Burger King Brands, Inc. MONOPOLY® & ©2005 Hasbro, Inc., used with permission. Silly Putty® is a registered trademark of Binney & Smith.

Cataloging in Publication Data
Szpirglas, Jeff
        They did what?! : your guide to weird & wacky things people do / Jeff Szpirglas ;
illustrated by Dave Whamond.

Includes index.
ISBN 1-897066-22-8 (bound). — ISBN 1-897066-23-6 (pbk.)

        1. Popular culture. 2. Curiosities and wonders. I. Whamond, Dave II. Title.

AG243.S98 2005   306   C2005-900861-X

Design & art direction: Claudia Dávila
Illustrations: Dave Whamond

We acknowledge the financial support of the Canada Council for the Arts, the Ontario Arts Council, the Government of Canada through the Book Publishing Industry Development Program (BPIDP), and the Government of Ontario through the Ontario Media Development Corporation's Book Initiative for our publishing activities.

ONTARIO ARTS COUNCIL
CONSEIL DES ARTS DE L'ONTARIO

Printed in Hong Kong

A   B   C   D   E   F

CONTENTS

A Note to the Reader

Aren't you glad to be a member of the species *Homo sapiens*? Think of the amazing things you can do every day that no other creature can accomplish: you tie your shoelaces, brush your teeth, make your bed, wash the dishes, take out the trash...the list is endless, according to my mother.

Our achievements throughout history are remarkable: we've built the Great Pyramids, walked the surface of the Moon, and invented computers that make it possible for writers to type words like the ones you're reading right now (and spell-check them, too!).

But for every one of our great accomplishments, we've made an even greater number of mistakes. Nobody celebrates those. Why is that?

We may live in a world that frowns upon flubs, but I'll let you in on a secret: some blunders are beneficial. How would you know not to lick a metal pole in the middle of January if some brave kid hadn't taught us all a lesson by freezing his tongue to one? It's time to celebrate all of the tongue-to-frozen-pole folks out there. Trying something different and unusual for its own sake can reveal amazing insights about the universe we live in. It can also leave you tongue-tied outside in the freezing weather.

If you're the least bit curious to learn about museums featuring nothing but toilet seats, the best April Fools' Day pranks, swimmers who frolic in frigid water, or a man who dangles live rattlesnakes from his mouth, then turn the page and reek on.

Jeff

("Reek on?" Whoops! That should be "read on."
Looks lake my smell-checker is broke in.
Oh, just turn the page and reek the book.)

April Fools' Day

A day dedicated to practical jokes? What a great idea! Since there are so many side-splitting stories about April 1st pranks, they have their own section in this book. See page 64 for an in-depth look at April Fools' greatest hits.

Far-Out Fads...

EVERYONE LOVES A FAD. ONE PERSON DOES SOMETHING NEAT AND DIFFERENT, LIKE WEARING HIS PAJAMA PANTS TO SCHOOL. SOON, A FEW OTHERS TRY IT OUT. BEFORE YOU KNOW IT, EVERYONE IS WEARING THEIR SLEEPWEAR TO SCHOOL...EVEN THE TEACHERS! FADS MAY COME AND GO, BUT SOME SEEM PARTICULARLY WORTHY OF REMEMBERING AGAIN.

Go Stuff It!

The telephone booth: if you're on the go and without a cell phone, it can be a lifesaver. But back in the late 1950s, the telephone booth was also fodder for fads. In South Africa, England, Canada, and the United States, one of the most tangled crazes was the art of telephone-booth stuffing. Booth-stuffing? It is just what it sounds like. You simply had to cram as many people as you could into a telephone booth. Different places had different rules. For example, one rule specified that the phone booth merely had to have a phone in it; another rule stated that you had to actually be able to place a call.

All right, students, is everyone ready to learn more about wacky fads?

Professor

Uh, teach? This is a book, not school. There's no one here but me.

Right, but I'm sure everyone reading the book would like to know that cramming isn't just for phone booths. People have been cramming into small cars since the late 1950s, too. Up to 57 people at once have squeezed into one Volkswagen Beetle!

Student

The Goal of Pole

Telephone-booth stuffing may sound like a nightmare for anyone with a case of claustrophobia, but it's a far cry from the loneliness of flagpole-sitting. Yes, you read that right: flagpole-sitting. Though it was not a fad that involved masses of participants (it only involved one person sitting on a flagpole for a long period of time), it allowed plenty of spectators to watch someone sit. Back in the 1920s, the king of flagpole-sitting was ex-sailor Alvin "Shipwreck" Kelly, who sat atop a flagpole for over 13 hours. Some other people decided to try this (dangerous) stunt out for themselves, but Kelly later topped his own record by sitting atop a flagpole for a staggering 49 days!

A Fishy Fad

If you were a petshop owner in Boston in 1939, it would have been a great year for sales. It was then that a first-year student at Harvard University took on a pretty wacky dare: he swallowed a goldfish. Apparently, he'd seen this stunt done ten years earlier, and bragged that he'd done it before. The stunt received a lot of media coverage. Weeks later, other students were trying to top the goldfish-swallowing feat—with over twenty goldfish swallowed in a given sitting. One man from Indiana claimed to have swallowed a whopping 5,000! Goldfish-swallowing got so out of hand that there were health warnings issued, and measures taken to protect the fish. True, most goldfish are eaten by larger predators...just usually not by college kids. The fad was short-lived and was pretty well sunk by the following year.

What if...

Ouchy, mama!

...the latest fad was barracuda swallowing?

[...and More Fads]

I'm Jim Smith!

There are a lot of people named Jim Smith living in the world today. But there's only one "Jim Smith Society." Started in 1969 by—surprise!—Jim Smith of Camp Hill, Pennsylvania, the Jim Smith Society boasts over 1,800 members, and throws fun get-togethers for all the Jim Smiths around. How do you tell who's who? You simply call a Jim by his city first—Camp Hill Jim, Manhattan Jim, Dallas Jim...you get the idea. What if there is more than one Jim living in a particular city? The other Jim just adds an additional identifying nickname. Because Sevierville Jim's grandson ran cross-country in high school, he's known as Sevierville "Running" Jim. And don't worry, this isn't a boys-only club. There are female members also, such as Jim Ann, from Oklahoma.

Attack of the Flashers!

Fun fads are making a splash in the age of the Internet. One recent fad is the flash mob. Given instructions by email, a group of people will meet at a predetermined place and time to do something wacky together. So what exactly do flash mobs do? In New York, people have hung out in Central Park making bird noises, or gone to big department stores looking for rugs. In Berlin, people cheered and shouted into their cell phones. In Rome, a flash mob went into a bookstore and started asking the staff for titles that didn't exist.

Shiver Swimmers

For some people—even those who live near a frigid lake or body of water—New Year's Day is a time to slip into a bathing suit and go for a swim. People all around the world like to take the icy plunge, from Canada and the United States to Germany, Finland, and Korea. The Coney Island Polar Bear Club in New York, which holds swims every Sunday from November to April, has been around since 1903. They've even helped out some movie crews: when stuntmen didn't want to jump into cold water, club members were ready, willing, and able.

This Pet Rocks

Are you tired of getting up first thing in the morning to feed your cat or walk your dog? Sick of the responsibility? Hate scooping the poop? Then you just might be a candidate to own the easiest pet to take care of, the Pet Rock. Created by Gary Dahl and released in 1975, the Pet Rock was…well…just what the name said it was. It came packaged in a box with "air holes," and a helpful manual that even instructed owners how to teach their Pet Rocks to roll over and play dead. More importantly, it was a huge success—over 1.5 million people bought Dahl's packaged rocks before the fad hit rock bottom the following year.

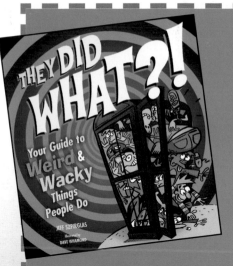

They Did WHAT?! is the world's first Pet Book!

Pet Book does not need food. You can take it on long walks, and it never needs to see a vet. Most importantly, you can learn a great deal from Pet Book by reading it from cover to cover. Take good care of it. Love it and it will love you back!

WARNING: Do not pet the sharp edges of the book. Paper cuts have been known to occur. Pet Book is allergic to water.

Fashion Faux-Pas

How to Wash Your Toga

Back in Ancient Rome, togas were the height of fashion. But what to do with a dirty toga? If you were wealthy enough, you could take your clothes to a fuller, or washerman. This washerman would coat the toga in clay to absorb the grease. And that's not all. The washerman would also soak fabric in stale urine from a public washroom. Apparently, this helped to thicken the cloth. Then the toga would be brushed, combed, and trimmed to smooth it out. And for the finishing touch: a final rinse with a spray of water from the washerman's mouth.

Non-Stink Underwear

The average human being breaks wind around 14 times a day. Finally, there's a revolutionary air-tight underwear, Under-Ease, to filter out our stinky scents. Featuring an "exit hole" with a filter that traps the smelly gases but allows the non-stinky gases to pass through, this underwear is washable and can last up to a year.

10

A Great Feat for Feet

Back in the 1300s, shoes were as much of a fashion statement as they are today, even if they didn't have brand names written on them, or endorsements from sports superstars. The shoe of the day, the poulaine (or piked shoe) was more befitting a clown than an athlete. When you slipped your feet into a pair of these, your toes would never reach the ends. Instead, these shoes continued for several inches past your toes before finally reaching a point. The ends of these big bananas had to be stuffed with moss or hair to keep them straight.

Talk about fancy footwork! To keep from pitching over, women who wore chopines almost always required the aid of servants to help them stagger about. Being helped around by servants showed people how rich chopine owners were (not to mention how uncomfortable their shoes were).

The Finer Points of Toe-Points

What do you know about a person from the length of his shoe? As shoes became more pointed, new laws restricted a person's shoe length, depending on how much money he had. One law stated that only shoes with toe-points up to 15 centimetres (6 inches) were allowed for a commoner, but a gentleman could wear his toe-points up to twice that length, and a nobleman up to four times that length or more!

Shoppin' for Chopines

Through the course of history, fashion has not only made shoes longer, but also taller. Thick-soled shoes called chopines were made fashionable in Venice in the 1400s. These decorated platform shoes for women were extremely difficult to walk about in. Some chopines rose over 60 centimetres (2 feet) from the ground!

It's All ON Your Head

WHAT BETTER PLACE TO MAKE A BOLD FASHION STATEMENT THAN ON THE TOP OF YOUR HEAD? THESE HAIR-RAISING FASHIONS ARE SURE TO TURN A HEAD OR TWO.

SCRITCH

SCRATCH

Wigged Out

In the 1600s when Louis XIV, the king of France, went bald, he took to wearing elaborate hairpieces. It didn't take long for wigs to catch on with the public—though expensive, they made brushing one's hair a thing of the past. By the late eighteenth century, wigs had really hit it big. A lady's hairdo could rise a metre (3 feet) above her head! Not only were they big, but designs often bordered on the bizarre. A wig might even be styled in the shape of a sailing vessel. Because wigs were so elaborate and difficult to manage, many were worn for weeks on end. The wig wasn't just a home for fashion—it often made a home for insects too, which would breed deep inside the false hair.

What if...?

...giant wig designs were in style today?

Hair to Wear

Barber Bill Black hates to see good hair go to waste. He's even created a plant fertilizer using hair as a main ingredient, which he calls FertHAIRlizer. But that's not all he's created from hair. Black has used human hair to weave an amazing array of clothing, including a hair tie, hair vests, and a hair shirt. Warm, yes, but the problem is that human hair can be itchier than a wool sweater.

Hats Off!

To see really crazy headwear in action, head to the Royal Ascot races, which are held every June in the English town of Ascot. Though the main attraction is the horse racing, the best view is from the stands...or, one might say, *of* the stands. Many female spectators compete by wearing the most extreme hat. One hat may resemble a lampshade, while another might look like a dartboard, and yet another like breakfast frying in a pan! And in case you're thinking of slapping on a baseball cap and trotting over to ogle the hats, be warned. It's fine to dress however you wish from the public enclosure, but if you're thinking of going to view the races from the Royal Enclosure, you can't show up if you're not dressed for the occasion. Men must wear respectable morning suits and ladies must wear hats, although they don't *have* to look like furniture or somebody's meal.

The Hat and the Elephant

Tilley Endurables is recognized as the maker of one of the world's most durable hats. How durable are they? Tilley salespeople will sometimes tell the true "elephant story." At the Bowmanville Zoo, a zookeeper had his Tilley hat eaten right off his head by an elephant. But not to worry, the hat later came out the elephant's other end completely intact—if a bit soiled. The zookeeper washed it off and put it back on. Since then, the elephant has eaten the same hat two more times! How durable is a Tilley hat? Apparently, the zookeeper wears the very same hat today.

Truly **Tall** Tales

YOU'RE AT SCHOOL AND YOUR FRIEND TELLS YOU A "WEIRD BUT TRUE" STORY THAT HE WAS E-MAILED. IT'S SUCH AN AMAZING STORY THAT YOU TELL YOUR FRIEND FROM ANOTHER SCHOOL, AND THEN SHE TELLS HER FRIEND.... SOON EVERYONE'S TALKING ABOUT THAT AMAZING TRUE STORY THAT WAS PROBABLY NEVER TRUE TO BEGIN WITH. DO ANY OF THESE FAMOUS "URBAN LEGENDS" SOUND FAMILIAR?

Gators in the Sewers

It's probably the mother of all North American urban legends: baby alligators from Florida, brought to New York City as cute pets, are flushed down the toilet once they get too big. These reptiles then grow and breed in the sewers. The lack of real subterranean saurians hasn't stopped the myth from growing, and working its way into newspapers, magazines, and movies. But despite the numerous stories, only one alligator was ever reportedly found in New York's sewers. In February 1935, three teenagers are said to have been shoveling snow into a manhole when they found a gator weighing in at 57 kilograms (125 pounds).

Scary Spider Stories

Spiders are everywhere in urban legends. A legend tells of a girl in the 1950s with a fashionable beehive hairstyle. One day, the girl passes out and is rushed to the hospital. There, a nurse finds an entire nest of deadly black widow spiders in the girl's hairdo! Another legend tells of a lady who hears a weird humming noise from her cactus, and notices that the plant often vibrates. When she calls the plant nursery to find out why, she is told to leave her house IMMEDIATELY. An emergency team comes over decked out in protective gear, brings the cactus to the backyard, and sets it on fire. Tons of deadly spiders scurry away.

...alligators were found not only in sewers, but also in bowls of soup?

One Costly Cookie

When a customer asks for the recipe of a department store's famous cookie, she is told that the store does not give it out. So the customer agrees to buy the recipe, for "two-fifty." Imagine the customer's surprise when her credit card statement comes a month later, and the charge for the recipe is listed as $250, not the $2.50 the customer presumed it would cost. And so the disgruntled customer sends an e-mail with the store's recipe to anyone who wants a copy for free. People always like a story where the underdog triumphs—but this one's not true.

The Mexican Pet

Here's yet another far-out-but-false story that has been circulated on the urban legend grapevine for around twenty years. A lady from California crosses the border into Mexico to go shopping for the day. Here, a number of stray dogs roam the streets. The lady gives one of the dogs some food, and the dog follows her around town all day. When it comes time to go home, the lady can't bear to leave her new friend behind. She sneaks the dog into her car by hiding it in some packages and manages to get both her and the dog safely across the border. That night she gives her new pet a bath and cleans it up, but the next day the dog is sick. The lady takes it to the vet, and she's forced to reveal how she got the dog. The vet tells her that it's not a dog she brought home, but a large sewer rat!

TOP FIVE "PETS" YOU SHOULD NEVER BRING HOME

5. Dust bunnies
4. A wasps' nest (especially if there are wasps in it)
3. Siberian tiger
2. Head lice
1. A box jellyfish*

*Sure, it looks harmless enough but it contains enough venom to kill 60 people. Don't invite one to your pool party.

Student

Believe It... Or Not!

LIKE THEIR COUSINS THE URBAN LEGENDS, THESE SUPPOSED "FACTS" ARE TOLD FROM PERSON TO PERSON. THEY OFTEN GET TOLD SO MANY TIMES THAT THEY'RE ACCEPTED AS FACTS, WHEN THEY COULDN'T BE FURTHER FROM THE TRUTH. PREPARE FOR SOME MONDO MISINFORMATION!

The Belief: Dropped food is safe if picked up within five seconds.

The Facts: Sometimes known as the "five-second rule," the idea is that a piece of food dropped onto the floor has a small window of time—five seconds—before the germs latch onto it. That idea's as dirty as the food that's been dropped on the floor. In 2003, a high school student from Illinois decided to test the theory herself. She treated floor tiles with bacteria. Then she tried placing cookies and candy on the tiles for up to five seconds. In every case, the bacteria were transferred to the food. By the way, the student also determined that junk food has a better chance of being retrieved from a dirty floor and eaten than healthy food does.

The Belief: Water going down a drain (like a sink or toilet) will rotate clockwise in the northern hemisphere and counter-clockwise in the southern hemisphere.

The Facts: People say this is due to the Coriolis force, which is caused by the Earth's rotation and which also influences the flow of air around the planet. The Coriolis force is certainly real, and explains things like why hurricanes rotate clockwise south of the equator and counter-clockwise north of the equator. But when it comes to the bathroom, the Coriolis force is so small in comparison to the other forces at work that it's not the one that determines the direction that the water drains.

A lot of people believe that Frankenstein is the name of a monster. The Facts: "Frankenstein" is actually the name of the monster's creator, Victor Frankenstein. In the original book written by Mary Shelley, the monster doesn't have a name! And just so you know, the monster is quite capable of carrying on an intelligent conversation and doesn't just stomp around grunting.

Professor

The Belief: Bulls hate seeing the color red.

The Facts: Well, considering that bulls are colorblind, they could very well hate purple, pink, and green, too. Nevertheless, a startling number of cartoons and movies depict bulls getting enraged at the sight of a matador waving a red cape at them. The fact of the matter is that bulls are quite irritable and aren't likely to take to the sound of a roaring crowd, or to having someone prance around waving any cape in front of them—regardless of the color.

The Belief: No two snowflakes are identical.

The Facts: The idea that every snowflake that has ever fallen is unique is a nice idea, but hard to swallow. Think for a moment of how much of the world gets snow, and how many years snow has been falling for. Admittedly, your own chances of successfully finding a matching pair of flakes are pretty slim, but there's hope! In 1988, a scientist from the National Center for Atmospheric Research was looking at some snow samples from Wisconsin and found...[pause for a drum roll]...two snow crystals that, while not identical, were very much alike!

The Belief: Drinking water cures the hiccups.

The Facts: Your diaphragm is a big wall of muscle that separates your lungs from your guts. A hiccup probably happens when the muscles of your diaphragm convulse and you gulp a bit of air. Your air passage quickly shuts, making the trademark sound of the hiccup. It's been estimated that an average case lasts for 60 hiccups. The list of suggested cures for hiccups seems endless: hold your breath, breathe into a paper bag, get startled suddenly, or eat some sugar. But there is no one cure-all for this affliction. The facts: drinking water may or may not stop your hiccups, but it will make you less thirsty.

The Most Foolish Page of All

Have you ever woken up on a particular spring morning and had an older sibling tell you that school had been rained out when there wasn't a cloud in the sky? Or did your teacher give a sudden pop quiz on stuff you'd never studied, then snicker all the way through? Chances are, it was April 1st and you fell for an April Fools' Day prank. You're not alone. Here are a number of notable pranks.

Fishy Origins

There are many theories to explain the origin of April Fools' Day. One convincing tale is that in sixteenth century France, the New Year used to be celebrated during the beginning of spring. However, in 1564 a new calendar, the Gregorian calendar, came into use. The new New Year's Day was January 1st. But people still liked to celebrate in the spring, and so an April 1st celebration became a tradition. Some people liked to poke fun at those who were still celebrating the old New Year's, and one popular joke was to send someone a fish as a "New Year's gift." Eventually, the January 1st New Year's date was established, but so was the foolish tradition of an April 1st celebration. In time it spread beyond France to England, and across the Atlantic to America.

April Fools' Day Foolery

The Place: Newspapers in the United States

The Prank: In 1983, a newswire ran a story telling people that a history professor at Boston University had traced the origin of April Fools' Day to the time of the Roman empire. The professor maintained that the fools and jesters of Roman Emperor Constantine thought that they were being ignored and decided to organize. They petitioned to have Constantine allow one of them to be king for a day, and the amused Constantine decided to go for it. That day was April 1st, and the first king-for-a-day was named King Kugel. April Fools' Day was born. Many newspapers ran this story, but ended up feeling pretty foolish since it wasn't true—especially when you realize that Kugel is the name of a Jewish noodle dish.

An Australian Iceberg

The Place: Sydney Harbour, Australia

The Prank: In 1978, a tugboat came into Sydney Harbour, pulling behind it a giant iceberg. Highly successful businessman Dick Smith had told people he was going to tow an iceberg into the city all the way from Antarctica and chop it up to make refreshing ice cubes at a cost of ten cents per cube. The jig was up when it began to rain, washing foam and shaving cream that had covered this "iceberg," which was nothing more than a hunk of floating plastic. Smith had actually considered towing an iceberg in for real, but later figured that a fake one would make for a great April Fools' Day prank. He and a friend secretly built it overnight, and on April 1st, Smith had members of his staff phone newspapers and radio stations to let them know about the iceberg entering the harbor.

[...and More April Foolery]

The Parade's Gone By

The Place: New York City

The Prank: In 2000, newspapers, radios, and TV stations were sent a message telling them that the annual New York City April Fools' Day Parade would start at noon. It would consist of many strange floats, including a $10 billion float celebrating failed missions to the planet Mars. Two TV networks sent camera crews to the scene to see what the story was all about. They shouldn't have brought their cameras, because there was no parade. The mastermind behind this hoax had been announcing an April Fools' Day parade for 15 years, and has been pulling pranks on the media since the 1960s.

A Whopper of a Joke

The Place: Newspapers across the United States

The Prank: Left-handed people never seem to have it easy. If you're writing a school report with pencil, you're likely to smear the pencil lead across the page. And if you have to cut paper, there aren't always left-handed scissors kicking around. On April 1st, 1998, BURGER KING® took the left-handed world by storm with a huge full-page ad in a major newspaper to announce their latest menu item, the "Left-Handed" WHOPPER®. The announcement stated that the ingredients in this new sandwich were no different than the regular kind, but the condiments were rearranged to prevent being spilled by left-handed hamburger-eaters. Apparently, thousands of people came in to the restaurant that day to order the new left-handed sandwiches, while others requested the right-handed ones.

Hotheaded Hoax

The Place: Newsstands and magazine racks

The Hoax: In April 1995, a science magazine called *Discover* ran a story about a biologist who had discovered a new species of mammal living in Antarctica. The animals were described as rodent-like, with large bony plates on their heads that had the ability to grow hot enough to melt the ice. This allowed them to rapidly tunnel through the frozen landscape—hence their name: ice borers. Ice borers' main source of food was penguins, which they hunted by melting the ice underneath the penguins' feet. Then they would surround the penguins and eat them.

Professor

Do ice-boring rodents that hunt penguins sound a little far-fetched to you? If so, you're less gullible than many readers. *Discover* magazine received lots of letters about this story, and still gets mail from people who don't realize it was all a big April Fools' prank.

A Whole Lotta Hoaxes

It's reassuring when foolery occurs on April 1st so we know that the pranks played on us are in the spirit of April Fools'. But other times, elaborate pranks and hoaxes catch us off-guard throughout the year. It's time to get hoaxed!

One Giant Hoax

Here's one hoax that truly rocks. Back in 1868, a cigar-maker named George Hull bought a five-ton block of gypsum stone in Iowa. He had it secretly shipped to Chicago, where he had the stone carved into the 1,360 kilogram (3,000 pound), 3-metre (10-foot) tall statue of a man. Still on the sly, Hull shipped his "giant" to farmland in Cardiff, New York, and had the statue buried in a swamp. A year later, Hull asked some workers to dig a well right where the statue was buried. When workers uncovered it, rumors spread about a petrified giant. People came to see it from miles around. Hotels were booked; restaurants did fabulous business. And so did Hull, who charged admission to see the giant. But some scientists pointed out that there was no evidence that human flesh could be petrified. In December 1869, Hull admitted it was just one giant hoax.

What if...

...the workers hadn't noticed the giant?

Martian Invasion

In the 1930s, most homes had a radio, and most radio stations broadcasted dramatic shows. One of the most famous was the Mercury Theatre, whose star director was the young Orson Welles. In October 1938, the Mercury Theatre ran their production of a novel called *The War of the Worlds,* a story about an invasion of Earth from outer space. Welles knew that listeners were used to having their programs interrupted for breaking news stories, and that's the trick he pulled with this adaptation. The production treated the invasion as if it were a live newscast, with "reporters" on the scene in Grover's Mill, New Jersey. People listening around the country were fooled—and some were spooked. In the end, Welles apologized for scaring the living daylights out of a nation, but the publicity also helped land him a deal to make movies in Hollywood.

Moon Buffoonery

In 1835, the *New York Sun* was one of the leading newspapers in New York. For six days that August, the paper published a series of articles about new discoveries of life on the Moon. The reports claimed the Moon was inhabited by beavers that walked on two feet, and even a blue unicorn-like animal! But that's not all. The paper also reported that a species of hairy, winged creatures that looked like intelligent apes and spoke to one another, were also observed. Unfortunately, no winged apes or unicorns were found on the Moon's surface when astronauts first visited it 134 years later.

[...and Practical Jokes]

Surely You Jest

Back in the 1500s, royalty in Europe paid their comedians, called jesters, to keep them amused. Jesters were quick-witted, and the most daring often played their best jokes on the royals who paid for their service. One notable jester, a man named Scogan, worked for King Edward IV of England. Scogan often offended the king, and once failed to pay Edward back a sum of money. Finally, tired of his antics, the king sentenced Scogan to death. Before the sentence could be carried out, though, Scogan faked his own death and funeral. During the mock funeral, Edward forgave Scogan. Hearing this, Scogan popped out of his casket to thank the king.

When Fairies Don't Play Fair

In 1917, two English girls took photographs of themselves in a garden. But the photographs also revealed the presence of some tiny, winged friends—fairies! The pictures looked suspicious, without any blurred movements, as a photo of a flying bird or insect would have turned up. Still, people fell for this hoax, including Sir Arthur Conan Doyle, the author of famous books about the detective Sherlock Holmes! It was later revealed that the fairies were actually just paper cut-outs attached to the bushes.

COME SEE THE AMAZING BONASSUS!

MEET THE INCREDIBLE BACTARANUS!

Amazing Animals

In the 1820s, a "newly discovered animal" called the "Bonassus" was displayed to the public in England. It was described as having an elephant's head, an antelope's horns, and the rear of a lion. But it was actually nothing more than an American buffalo. The same exhibitor also had a "Bactaranus," an animal billed as having a lion's strength and an elephant's size. (It was a camel.) One of the most famous forgeries of the time was a "mermaid," also displayed in England. Reportedly, 300 to 400 people came daily to see this mummified mermaid. What were they actually staring at? The upper body of a monkey, with the skin and fins of a salmon all sewn together.

Apple Saws

Back in the 1800s, a rumor circulated that New York City was in deep trouble. The island of Manhattan was getting too heavy from too many buildings going up on one end, and it was feared that the heavy end might sink into the ocean. The solution? Saw the island of Manhattan in half, turn it around, then reattach the two halves so that the weight would be evenly distributed. The story goes that a man named Lozier took charge of the project and rounded up a number of people to help him. Huge saws, each a hundred feet long, had to be constructed. But on the day that the sawing was to commence, Lozier was nowhere to be found! In the end, some people must have wanted to saw Lozier in half for pulling such a huge hoax. Because there are so few sources to back this story up, it may not have been a real hoax at all, but that other beast, an urban legend.

In the late 1700s, a creature brought to scientists in England was described as "an amphibious animal of the mole kind." With its furry body, webbed feet, beaver-like tail, and curious duck-like bill, it seemed it had to be a hoax. But after two more were brought to the British Museum, a scientist realized it was no fake—and England was introduced to the duck-billed platypus of Australia!

Professor

The *Extreme* Sports Scene

PEOPLE THRILL AT COMPETITIVE SPORTS — THE CROWDS, THE EXCITEMENT, THE ATHLETES PUSHING THEIR LIMITS. BUT THE SPORTS ON THESE PAGES *REALLY* TAKE SPORTS TO THE EXTREME. SO STRAP ON YOUR HELMET, BE A GOOD SPORT, AND ENJOY.

Pressed and Steamed— to the Extreme!

Do household chores bore you? Are you sick of having to iron the creases out of your pants? Fret no more, there's a new sport that's im*pressing* itself on the world: extreme ironing. This sport began in 1997, when a man from Leicester, England, decided to combine his hobby of rock climbing with impending household chores. Extreme ironing is now practiced all around the world, and in some pretty wild places. Garments have been pressed 16 metres (52 feet) under the North Sea, and as high as 5,895 metres (19,340 feet) high, on Mount Kilimanjaro in Africa. There are even extreme ironing championships, and ironers can compete for the famed Rowenta Trophy. How long will it be before this new sport becomes an Olympic event (especially if the athletes promise to iron the clothes of the members of the International Olympic Committee)?

Bathtubs Ahoy!

In 1967, over 200 competitors raced in the harbor at Nanaimo, British Columbia. But they weren't racing boats—they were racing bathtubs. Since then, Nanaimo has hosted the annual "Great" International World Championship Bathtub "Race." Most bathtubs aren't made to float, so the models used by racers combine wood and fiberglass, modeled after an old-style tub. Simply finishing the race is an achievement. Motors powering the tubs have stalled; boats have broken apart and even sunk. Large boats patrol the race in case of trouble, but it's a huge celebration nonetheless.

Race You to the Bathroom

If you think it's strange to race a bathtub, how about racing an entire bathroom? Every September, the Great Klondike International Outhouse Race and Scavenger Hunt offers contestants the chance to race an actual outhouse through Dawson City, Yukon. This race requires a real team effort—four people to push the outhouse on wheels, and one person to sit in it. Outhouses can be built or rented, and they usually have fun names, like the Whizzer of Oz.

Paddle Your Pumpkin

Racing bathroom objects not your style? A similarly challenging event in Windsor, Nova Scotia, involves contestants racing mammoth, hollowed-out pumpkins—which can weigh between 225 and 410 kilograms (500 and 900 pounds)—across a lake. Usually two to three pumpkins sink every year—most often because the tops of the pumpkins were cut off too low, allowing them to easily fill with water. Sink or swim, one thing's for sure: there are enough pumpkin seeds to go around for everyone.

[Being a Good Sport—Part 2]

To Zorb or Not to Zorb

If you have a penchant for somer-saulting down grassy hills, you might want to step into a Zorb and try the same feat. What's a Zorb, you ask? Developed in New Zealand, and now popular around the world, it's essentially like being in a giant hamster ball that rolls down a hill. Once inflated (usually by a leaf blower), and once you're safely strapped in, the Zorb is sent rolling down a hill, taking you with it at speeds of up to 50 kilometres (31 miles) per hour—the speed limit on most city streets. Because the Zorb rotates only once for every 10 metres (33 feet) that it rolls, it won't even make you feel like losing your lunch.

Cheesed Off

Each year, for at least 200 years, residents of Cooper's Hill, England, have held an annual cheese-rolling contest. What's "cheese-rolling," you ask? First you need a hunk of Gloucester cheese. Then you need a nice, steep hill—Cooper's Hill, to be precise. When everybody's ready, the cheese is rolled down the hill, and the contestants race down after it at full speed. There's lots of falling and tumbling, and not just by the cheese. As for the grand prize-winner? He or she gets to keep the cheese.

In 2003, there was a break with tradition when the Cooper's Hill cheese-rolling contest was canceled due to an earthquake!

Professor

28

Bogged Down

Llanwrtyd Wells in Wales is the smallest town in Britain. It's also the home of the World Bog Snorkeling Championships. Most people go snorkeling for the chance to see gorgeous underwater vistas and fascinating marine life. But, though marine life is certainly plentiful—including water scorpions and other bugs—the bog-snorkeling championships don't give the swimmer much visibility. Each year, contestants venture out to a 55-metre (180-foot) long, 1-metre (3-foot) deep trench that's been cut in the swampy Waen Rhydd peat bog. Contestants have to don their masks, snorkels, and flippers, then swim two lengths without using regular swimming strokes. The person with the fastest time emerges the winner (and also emerges quite slimy). Competitors have traveled from all over the world, including Europe, Australia, and North America. Many people don wet suits for this stinky task, although contestants have been known to wear body paint, business suits, and even ballet tutus.

A Spec-toe-cular Event

It all started back in 1976 at Ye Olde Royal Oak Inn in Wetton, England, where locals were trying to come up with a new sport that no one else knew about. That's when toe-wrestling was born! Though the early contests died out, toe-wrestling was revived in 1990 when the inn's landlord found the old rules and decided to bring the "sport" to the masses. By 1994, the World Toe Wrestling Championships had become an annual event. Here's how to play the game: players must keep their non-wrestling feet off the ground, but their bums always have to be on the floor. The wrestling feet (socks off) are inserted into a toe rack (standing on a platform known as a toe-dium), which keeps the heels from slipping all over the place. Big toes are interlocked, and when the referee gives the word, players try to force their opponent's foot off the toe rack. Whoever wins the first two matches out of three emerges the toe-tal winner.

Student

TOP FIVE OTHER SPORTS THAT COULD TAKE PLACE IN A BOG

5. Bogging for Leeches
4. Synchronized Bog Swimming
3. Bog-sketball
2. Bog Figure Skating (when the bog freezes over)
1. Bog White Water Rafting (rapids required)

Creature Comforts

In our quest for comfort, we can certainly go overboard with designer beds, TV remotes, and expensive beauty products. But we humans don't just like to pamper ourselves — we also go to great lengths for the furry friends in our lives.

The Mayoral Mutt

In the state of California the vote for mayor went to the dogs! In 1981, in the small community of Sunol, a black labrador-rottweiler mix named Bosco beat out two human candidates for the position of honorary town mayor. Bosco kept his lofty position for around ten years, and could be seen leading downtown parades and marches, wearing a vest and badge.

Horsepower

Two thousand years ago, Roman Emperor Caligula was a ruler who really liked his horse, Incitatus. It seems that this lucky horse was given an ivory manger, a marble stall, purple blankets, and a collar of precious stones. Some stories indicate that Caligula invited Incitatus to banquets, and even tried to give his horse political power. Talk about horsepower!

When Pets Get Married

When wedding bells rang for Phet and Ploy, two cats (yes, cats!) from Thailand, it was an extravagant affair. Five hundred guests attended, and the two cats arrived by helicopter and limousine. A parrot was best man and an iguana the maid of honor for this happy feline pair.

Away with the Litterbox

A lion may be the king of beasts, but this throne is strictly for house cats—and may make litterboxes a thing of the past. But there's a catch: cat owners will have to share their toilets with their feline companions. The hottest seat in the feline kingdom is the CatSeat™, which is fastened to a toilet seat so kitties get used to using the same one as you. Next thing you know they'll be wearing your slippers and bathrobe!

Cat Flap

In London, England, a former feline stray named Tinker found himself an elderly owner. She died in 2002, but Tinker was one cat who didn't get the boot. It turns out that Tinker's owner was so fond of him that in her will she left her three-bedroom house and a nice inheritance to the cat. But there's a catch: if Tinker ever has enough of the high life and decides to leave this lap of luxury, the house goes to the (human) neighbors.

Flag This Down!

Your favorite furry friend sometimes needs to get somewhere, and so far hasn't learned to drive the family car. What to do? Call Pet Taxi. In the continental United States, there's a taxi service that caters to critters, and will drive them to the vet, the groomer, or even to the airport. Pet Taxi has also saved the lives of a few dogs in need by quickly rushing them to the vet. This service isn't just for dogs and cats—even baby sharks and large turtles have hopped aboard for a drive through town.

Drive-Thru Dining

Let's say you're in the car and your dog has to eat on the go. If you're in Niles, Michigan, you could make a stop at the Doggie-Drive-Thru®. Yes, now there's an actual drive-through that provides healthy foods for dogs and cats...and even people. Much of the menu consists of treats made up to look like burgers and pretzels. And if your pooch is in party mode, Doggie-Drive-Thru also caters dog birthday parties, and can provide party hats, loot bags, and Frosty Paws, a cold doggie dessert.

Is it too late to super-size the dog food?

[Creature Comforts, Too]

Hotel de Pet

The America Dog and Cat Hotel knows how to create a luxury pet experience. Oriental rugs are laid out on the floors, animal-themed paintings are hung on the walls, and there's the smell of potpourri in the air. In addition to chew toys, there are TVs and relaxing music. Cats can chill out in three-story kitty condos, with beds, expensive lamps, and mini TVs. Best of all is the free-range area where the animals can mingle. If it sounds so good that you're thinking of checking yourself in, just remember that for the free-range run, visitors must have had their shots and been spayed or neutered.

A Bed Fit for a Cow

Is your bed not giving you the support you need? Are you tossing and turning from discomfort all night? Do you like to drink milk? If you answered "yes" to any of those questions, you might want to mosey on over to a dairy farm for the night, and join those cows out there who are kicking back in comfort. They've got waterbeds! The cow waterbed consists of two layers of strong rubber with a compartment in between filled with water. When the cow lies down for a snooze, the bedding takes on the cow's shape. Some farmers have discovered that their well-rested, comfy cows can end up producing more milk.

Squirrel City

If you're a squirrel, preferably a black squirrel, the place you'd probably most want to call home is Marysville, Kansas. As you head into town, you'll see signs announcing "Marysville, Kansas—Black Squirrel City." There's a black squirrel anthem and an annual celebration for these rodents. Apparently, there weren't any black squirrels in Marysville until either the 1800s or the 1920s (depending on who tells the story), but they're making up for lost time now. Black squirrels have the right-of-way on the streets and railroad crossings, and they can trespass anywhere they like. If you harm one, even accidentally, there's a $25 fine. It's a squirrel's life!

Diapers Fit for a Bird

Now, finally, pet birds can be liberated from their cages. If your pet bird wants out, you might think about investing in the FlightSuit™, a bird diaper. This product looks like a pair of coveralls that fits over a bird's body and fastens behind the wings, allowing the ploppy bird to keep its legs and wings free to flap about. The actual diaper has a patented poop pouch that collects bird droppings and keeps the stinky splashes away from the bird's body. These aren't Just for exotic birds like parakeets and macaws. There are sizes that fit pigeons and doves used by magicians, as well as a line of diapers for farm animals like ducks, geese, and chickens. The possibilities for bird diapers seem endless....

...the exercising turkeys released a workout video?

Turkeys and Treadmills

We've spent a lot of time discussing how humans like to let animals lounge about and enjoy the finer things in life. But sometimes animals need a little exercise, too. In 1996, at Harvard University, researchers put some wild turkeys onto treadmills. The researchers were trying to investigate the effect of exercise on animals. For this science experiment, some turkeys had to huff and puff on the treadmill each day over the summer and into early autumn, while another group sat around—so the fit ones could be compared to the idle ones. No word yet on whether the researchers have signed the turkeys up for aerobics or yoga classes.

Are You Going to Eat That?

PEOPLE AROUND THE WORLD EAT ALL SORTS OF THINGS. BUT NO MATTER WHERE YOU LIVE, THERE ARE FOODS THAT PUSH THE ENVELOPE. THEY'RE WEIRD, THEY'RE UNUSUAL, AND WHO KNOWS...THEY MAY BE TASTY.

Ultimate Leftovers

Around 36,000 years ago, a steppe bison was killed by lions near Fairbanks, Alaska. The half-eaten animal ended up buried in the frozen earth, the cold temperature of the permafrost keeping the meat from going bad. Years and years later—in 1979—its foot was spotted sticking out of the ground, and the bison was exhumed and stored in a freezer. The meat that was left clinging to its bones was still red and smelled like a combination of beef and dirt. In April of 1984, scientists decided to cook some of the frozen meat in a stew. They were the first modern people to eat a bison from the Pleistocene era (1.8 million years ago to 10,000 years ago). Amazingly, it tasted "agreeable," according to one of the people who tried it.

Mummy in the Tummy

Thousands of years ago, ancient Egyptians made mummies to preserve the bodies of their dead. Years later, people dug up the mummies and found them coated with a black, tar-like goop, which they thought was something called bitumen. During the twelfth century, some people claimed that bitumen could be used as a medicine. Mummies were dug up and ground into medicinal powder. This "powdered mummy" was used for treating cuts, coughing, headaches, and stomachaches. But not only did mummies lack bitumen, eating "medicinal mummy" could cause bad breath, cramps, and vomiting.

Don't Sweat It

How would you feel about topping a heated game of soccer off by gulping down a can of Pocari Sweat? It's a Japanese sports beverage, but don't worry, it doesn't contain any actual sweat. The name may sound unusual, but the drink contains ingredients found in a human's own body fluids, like sodium and potassium, which you sweat away in a given day, especially when exercising for long periods of time.

Fizzy and Feathered

Turkey and gravy is a Thanksgiving staple, but it's most often enjoyed served hot on a plate so you can chew each tender morsel. Well, chew no more! Now this traditional dish has become a soda pop flavor. In 2003, the Jones Soda Co. released "Turkey & Gravy Soda," and it sold remarkably well. Six thousand bottles of the stuff sold out on the Jones Soda website within three hours. On a different website, there were bids for a staggering $63 per bottle! The company has created other unusual soda flavors, too, such as canned ham and fish taco. It's hard to know if you should feel hungry or thirsty....

TOP FIVE SODA FLAVORS WE'D LIKE TO SEE

5. Bold Baloney
4. Blue Cheese in a Bottle
3. Asparagus Adventure
2. Lip-Smacking Liver
1. Fish Stick Surprise

[...and More Fun with Food]

What a lovely, elegant dinner!

Mind Your Manners

Rules for good table manners have been around for years. An ancient Egyptian set, called "The Instructions of Ptahhotep," was probably written around the twentieth century B.C.E. (long, long ago). Guides from around the thirteenth century also outlined good table manners. Among the rules that should be followed: snorting, spitting, and smacking the lips were frowned upon. One guide mentioned that it was bad to blow one's nose on a tablecloth or pick at your teeth with a knife. And by the way...that still holds true today!

Nutty Napkin Nonsense

At some point in the Middle Ages, some people stopped wiping their mouths on tablecloths and used smaller pieces of linen to keep their hands and faces clean. Enter the napkin! Early napkins were pretty big, since people still used their hands to eat and tended to get messy in a hurry. For a truly refined meal, folding the napkin neatly was an art form unto itself. One banquet from sixteenth century Rome apparently had napkins folded around live birds. When the guests opened up their napkins, the birds flew away, hopefully before making a mess of them!

Stylin' Food

How often do you drool when you see a TV commercial for a juicy flame-grilled burger with crisp green lettuce and bright red tomatoes? If you knew what you might be looking at, your mouth could go dry. Most advertisers hire "food stylists," who make food look fresh and tasty all day long. Because a commercial takes many hours to shoot, a burger may not look as appealing as the day wears on. Sometimes beef patties are only slightly burned so that the insides are still raw (to make them look fresh). Smearing the patty with Vaseline gives it a shine. Cardboard or plastic wrap could be used to separate the lettuce and tomatoes and keep them from getting soggy. Extra sesame seeds might even be glued onto the bun. Ice cream is another food that gets a similar makeover. Since it would melt into a gloopy puddle under hot studio lights, often scoops of vegetable shortening or mashed potatoes sit in for the real thing. By substituting these products, the advertiser doesn't have to needlessly waste food.

Fun with Fingers

Are you tired of being told how to eat your food? Well, fret no longer! There are a few things that even royalty are allowed to eat with their fingers. Asparagus can be eaten without utensils—as long as it isn't smeared with sauce and the stalks aren't too mushy. (By the way, polite rules don't allow you to dangle two pieces from your mouth and tell people that you are the rare and endangered "asparagus walrus.") With corn on the cob, a fork and knife would just be silly. But you're only supposed to butter your corn a few rows at a time and eat across the cob in a straight line, like an old-fashioned typewriter. No need to let out a "ding" when you reach the end of the row!

Adventures in
Adventising

ADVERTISEMENTS HAVE BEEN AROUND FOR ABOUT AS LONG AS HUMANS HAVE HAD PRODUCTS OR SERVICES TO SELL. TO GRAB YOUR ATTENTION, COMPANIES WILL MAKE FLASHY COMMERCIALS OR FEATURE FUNKY PROMOTIONS. HERE ARE A FEW OF HISTORY'S QUIRKIER ADVERTISING STORIES AND CAMPAIGNS.

Staging a Publicity Stunt

A press agent named Jim Moran orchestrated some of the silliest publicity stunts around, and his wacky ideas were always making the news, from the 1930s to his retirement in the 1980s. For example, Moran donned an ostrich costume and personally sat on an ostrich egg for over 19 days until it hatched to promote the film *The Egg and I.* For another publicity stunt, he was paid to see how difficult it was to find a needle in a haystack. Moran was presented with a 3.7-metre (12-foot) haystack in which a single needle had been placed, and found the needle over 80 hours later. Finding a needle in a haystack isn't the only famous phrase that Moran tried out for real. He also led a bull into a china shop in New York...but the bull didn't even break one dish! It was a disappointing day for the media, but a happy one for the china shop.

When Names Get Tired

Sometimes in advertising, it's all about having the right name. In one publicity campaign, Dunlop Tires offered money to people with the last name of Dunlop. The catch? They had to change their last name to Dunlop-Tire. And four Dunlops in Canada legally changed their surnames. Now their signatures are four letters longer, and they're each $6,000 richer! No stranger to strange publicity campaigns, Dunlop has also had events featuring sumo wrestlers, belly-flop contests, and even had 100 people roll tires down the streets of Toronto.

The Pudding Guy

When David Phillips (a.k.a. "The Pudding Guy") saw a promotion from Healthy Choice food company offering customers 500 frequent flyer miles for every 10 product codes mailed in, he quickly filled his shopping cart with Healthy Choice soup. He then drove to supermarkets around town and bought enough pudding cups to fill a van. By the promotion deadline, David had spent over $3000 on Healthy Choice products. He donated most of the food to charity, but he ended up receiving enough frequent flyer miles for around 50 round trip flights anywhere in the United States, and 30 to Europe!

A Very Little Land Grab

In the 1950s, a popular radio show about a Royal Canadian Mounted Police officer who fought crime in the Yukon Territory was adapted into a television show. An advertiser came up with an idea for a breakfast cereal company to get in on the action. The plan was to give away land in the Yukon. The cereal company paid $1,000 for a plot of land near the old gold prospecting town of Dawson. They divided their land up into 21 million plots that were each one square inch. Deeds to these tiny pieces of land were placed into boxes of the cereal, advertising the tiny chunks of real estate as "FREE Gold Rush Land." As it turned out, the ad campaign was like hitting gold, and those 21 million boxes were bought within weeks. But there was a problem. The company failed to pay the property taxes, and ten years later, the land was seized back over an unpaid bill of $37.20. For a long time, those deeds of land were worthless, but today they're valued as collector's items!

LAND DEED 1" All Yours!

WELCOME TO THE
YUKON TERRITORY

Spare No Expense

Money is useful to have around when you need to buy important things, like food and clothes. But what if you had millions to spend? If you've got money to burn—or if you just want to imagine what it would be like—here are some ideas....

Fancy a game of Monopoly®?

Toying with Wealth

Maybe you're a fun-loving person, and you'd like to invest in some fun stuff. How about a board game? San Francisco jeweler Sidney Mobell's version of Monopoly® comes complete with a playing board made of gold. Even the game pieces—including the houses, hotels, and the dice—are gold! There are a total of 156 gemstones set into the board and pieces, so if you ever play Mobell's Monopoly, be sure not to lose any of the pieces under the sofa. The set is valued at around $2 million!

Professor

Board games aren't the only thing Mobell has turned into a luxury item. His other works include a solid gold mousetrap (with a diamond wedge of cheese) and a gold baby pacifier, complete with eight diamonds!

Golden Bathroom

If you're passing through Hong Kong, you might want to make a pit stop at the 3-D GOLD Tourism Exhibition Hall. It's not just the jewelry that's worth eyeing there. Store-owner Lam Sai Wing invested more than $4 million in the store's bathroom, which is literally gleaming with gold. There are golden tiles and sinks...and, yes, even the toilet is made out of solid gold (and so is the toilet brush that's used to clean it). To spruce the place up with some color, the ceiling features glittering rubies and emeralds.

That's Sweet!

Some sweets have been to far-away places and have claimed some far-out prices. In 2001, a chocolate bar that went on Robert Scott's Antarctic expedition in the early 1900s was auctioned off for $710! At that same sale, a biscuit from Sir Ernest Shackleton's attempted Antarctic crossing (1914–16) went for 7,637 British pounds ($11,383)! Think how many regular—and not stale!—cookies you could get for that price.

Hordes of Hair

Hair is a resource famous people (who aren't bald) can keep on producing, and it can certainly fetch a mint. That's what happened in 2002, when a bunch of hair that belonged to Elvis Presley, the king of rock 'n' roll, was sold in an on-line auction. Clumped together, the hair was about as big as a baseball. Elvis's personal barber of over 20 years collected the giant hairball, and it was worth the wait—the hair sold for more than $100,000!

Strange Museums

What comes to mind when you read the word "museum?" Dinosaurs? Ancient Egyptian mummies? Suits of armor? Priceless works of art? How about bananas, toilet seats, and cockroaches? Didn't think you'd find them in a museum? Read on...and think again.

Oh! I've been spotted.

YES! We have bananas!

Go Bananas!

Ken Bannister was attending a boring business convention in 1972 when he decided to brighten everyone's day by handing out yellow banana stickers to the attendees. People at the convention enjoyed the idea, and started sending Bannister banana items in the mail. Ken's collection grew over the years, and in 1976, he opened the world's biggest banana museum in Altadena, California. Today the museum has over 17,000 items on display and is divided into sections. The "soft" section features plush banana toys, a banana tent, and even a banana couch, while the "hard" section features lead, brass, and, yes, cement bananas. There's even a petrified banana that's been kicking around since 1975 (found after five years in a closet). So far, nobody has slipped on any banana peels when entering the museum.

A Home for Awful Art

In 1992, an antique dealer found a framed picture in a trash can. Thinking the frame might be worth a few bucks, he carefully picked it out and discovered why the picture had been tossed. It was a bizarre portrait of an old woman floating over a field of daisies. It was so bad it was good, and the antique dealer knew he was onto something. With a friend's help, he established the Museum of Bad Art in Dedham, Massachusetts. The museum, which opened in the fall of 1993, features art that is "too bad to be ignored." Featured works include an evil clown and a portrait of a man sitting on a toilet, and the museum is always looking for new art to display. But be warned: this "bad art" museum rejects most of the artwork sent to it for not being bad enough. The museum is really looking for artists who tried, but failed with spectacular results.

Ken Bannister also founded the International Banana Club®, which boasts members from over 25 countries and even hands out banana degrees, such as a Masters or Doctorate in Bananistry to club members who earn banana merit points.

How does that rate against a Mustard Doctor (MD) degree?

King of Condiments

If you really like to lay on the mustard when dressing up a hot dog, then you might want to stop by the Mount Horeb Mustard Museum in Wisconsin. Lawyer Barry Levenson has created a museum devoted entirely to one of the world's oldest condiments, dating back to the time of the ancient Egyptians. Visitors can view over 4,000 kinds of mustard from countries all around the world, including Sri Lanka, Israel, and China. There's even an educational "Mustard-piece Theater" video and displays of vintage mustard pots and advertisements. Levenson also offers "courses" to students, such as the Sociology of Mustard. Pass enough courses and you could earn your very own MD (Mustard Doctor degree).

Flush with Art

What happens when a man decides to combine art and a career in plumbing? For over 35 years, Barney Smith has been creating amazing works of art. But unlike many painters, his medium is not canvas, but the toilet seat lid. It started in 1970 when Smith mounted a set of deer antlers onto a toilet seat lid. He now has created over 720 different works of toilet seat art and displays them at the appropriately named Barney Smith Toilet Seat Art Museum in Texas, which opened in 1992.

Professor

Student

Funny Festivals

Need a reason to celebrate? It seems there's no limit to the kinds of things that people find to feel festive about. Try some of these on for size.

Charming Worms

Are you just a pretty face—or do you have what it takes to charm earthworms right out of the ground? Since 1980, the World Worm Charming Championships have been held in Nantwich, England. This annual festival sees competitors trying to coax worms from a plot of earth, using whatever charms they can muster. Some try blaring music or tap dancing to lure those wrigglers up, but usually, the vibrations from a garden fork work best. The person who charms the most worms at the end of 30 minutes wins the coveted Golden Worm Trophy, and a silver trophy is given to the person who raises the heaviest worm. The record for most worms charmed was set early on by a man who managed to lure 511 out of the ground!

...there were Great White Shark Charming Competitions?

Meanwhile, Back at the Bug Bowl

If you have a thing for insects, you may want to check out the Bug Bowl at Purdue University in Indiana. Don't miss the excitement of the "All-American Trot," a live cockroach race that takes place on the Roachill Downs track. Jockeys compete for the "Old Open Can," a bronze garbage can with a cockroach on top. Though some of the games may seem silly, the Bug Bowl does give people a taste of the role insects play in nature. It gives them a taste of insects, too—in the form of cookies, cakes, and other buggy treats.

Rock 'n' Roll 'n' Air

Have you ever put on a rock album and wished it was you who was playing that blistering guitar solo to a huge stadium crowd? If so, you're not alone. Every year since 1996 the Air Guitar World Championships, which promote both peace on Earth and rocking out, are held at the Oulu Music Video Festival in Finland. The rules are pretty simple: each contestant gets on stage to perform two one-minute selections from a rocking tune—one they choose and one chosen by the event organizers. The contestant's instrument must be invisible, but it can be either a non-existent acoustic or electric guitar. Contestants pick up points for things like artistic merit, originality, charisma, and..."airness." Think you've got what it takes? Better crank up your stereo and start practicing.

A Festival of Poop

Animal droppings make for great crop fertilizer, and are rich in nutrients that most growing plants need. When residents of Desmond, Ontario, were trying to raise money to fix up a one-room red schoolhouse, they asked themselves what they had to offer people. A whole lot of poop, that's what: chicken poop, cow poop, horse poop, pig poop, sheep poop. Recognizing the importance of poop, they organized a festival celebrating animal droppings, called Manurefest. Scooping that poop was like hitting a gold mine. Once properly composted, bags of manure sold well, and there was even a "premium poop" blend of sheep and horse manure sold. Desmond is still proud to be the manure capital of Ontario, and perhaps the world.

Invasion of the Duckies!

It all started in Arizona. Rubber ducks were "adopted" by residents and raced down a river to raise money for charity. Today, rubber-duck racing has become a worldwide phenomenon, most notably in Singapore, where the Great Singapore Duck Race has been held annually since 1998. When race day comes, a huge dump truck packed with the adopted rubber ducks backs up to the Singapore River and dumps them in. Over 123,000 ducks were loaded into the river in 2002—a world record!

A Page of
Daring Devils

There's good reason to fear certain activities—it's a basic mechanism for survival. Yet there always seems to be a few individuals who face the fear and attempt foolhardy feats. DO NOT attempt any of this at home, but you may enjoy reading about these extreme exploits.

Motorcycle Master

Robert Craig Knievel, better known as Evel Knievel, knows a few interesting places to ride a motorcycle. In the mid-1960s, he started performing daring motorcycle feats. Why take the easy road when you can ride through walls of fire or jump over vehicles? Evel's biking beginnings saw him jumping over live rattlesnakes, but Knievel worked his way up to more formidable challenges. Using a ramp, a motorbike, and a lot of guts, Knievel jumped over 19 parked cars in 1971, then jumped over 52 stacked cars in 1973. Two years later, he cleared 14 buses. But the life of a daredevil has its downside, too: Knievel broke 35 bones, before eventually retiring in 1980.

Mr. Knievel's motorcycle is on display at the Smithsonian Institute in Washington, and there's even a river named after him in the state of Arkansas.

Spectacular Stunts

With Hollywood special effects getting better and better, many movie stunts are assisted by computers. But in the early days of filmmaking, stars, such as silent comedian Buster Keaton, often performed their own stunts. One of the most impressive stunts in Keaton's career took place in his movie *Steamboat Bill, Jr.* (1928). In that film, the wall of a house falls on top of Keaton, who is only saved from being flattened because he's standing at the exact position where the open window falls (with only a tiny space on either side of him). You probably won't be surprised to learn that his godfather was none other than the late, great escape artist Harry Houdini.

Falling for Niagara Falls

The spectacular Niagara Falls, divided by the U.S./Canada border, have seen a lot of daredevil activity. They may look pretty, but the Horseshoe Falls (on the Canadian side) aren't gentle. The water travels over the falls at 109 kilometres per hour (68 miles per hour) into whirlpool rapids below. You'd think that with such rushing waters people would steer clear of them. Not so! In 1901, Annie Taylor became the first person to go over the falls in a barrel (an airtight wooden one). In 1911, Bobby Leach tried the stunt in a steel barrel, emerging with only a pair of broken kneecaps and a busted jaw. Still, it's the lucky Niagara Falls daredevils who have lived to tell the tale.

Climb Every Skyscraper

Instead of falling hard and fast, a man named Alain "Spiderman" Robert climbs to great heights. He performs this amazing feat using only his bare hands to scale buildings, despite two serious accidents that left him with vertigo and a doctor's report telling him he'd never climb again. Fat chance! Since then, Robert has climbed over 70 skyscrapers all over the world, including the National Bank of Abu Dhabi in the United Arab Emirates, the Eiffel Tower in Paris, the Empire State Building in New York, and the Sears Tower in Chicago. He even dressed up as the famous comic-book character Spider-Man for his wall-crawling exploits.

The Sky's the Limit

IN 1903, THE WORLD WAS FOREVER CHANGED WHEN THE WRIGHT BROTHERS FLEW THE WORLD'S FIRST WORKING AIRPLANE. ALTHOUGH HUMANS AREN'T BORN WITH WINGS, WE ENJOY TAKING TO THE AIR, THROWING THINGS INTO IT...OR DROPPING THINGS FROM IT. HERE'S A SAMPLING OF SOME OF OUR OUTLANDISH AIRBORNE ANTICS.

A Not-So Bouncy Ball

In 1997, a man from Wales took on the task of creating the world's biggest rubberband ball. Six years—and six million rubberbands!—later, the man and his 1,180 kilogram (2,600 pound) rubber ball were flown to the United States to drop the ball in California's Mojave Desert. The ball was flown up to an altitude of 1,830 metres (6,000 feet). Once released, it flew through the air at 644 kilometres (400 miles) per hour for around 20 seconds, and then...BOOM! (Not BOING!) People were hoping that the ball would bounce, but instead it left a crater 0.9 metres (3 feet) deep and 2.7 metres (9 feet) in diameter.

A Toss-Up

Sure, you can toss a paper airplane into the air and marvel at the height and distance it goes. But what about throwing less aerodynamically sound objects, like...oh, say, a holiday fruitcake? It's been done. In fact, a fruitcake toss is held each year in Manitou Springs, Colorado. Here, you can toss that fruity holiday cake by hand or catapult...or you can even run a fruitcake-on-wheels down a ramp! And for some really extreme tossing, there's always the annual Punkin' Chunkin' Festival in Delaware. This celebration's highlight is the launching of that famous fall gourd, the pumpkin. Tractors are hooked up to rigging and specially designed cannons that rise nearly three stories into the air. Some launched pumpkins fly so powerfully that when they're fired out of their air cannons, they travel almost as fast as the speed of sound.

The Cannonball: Not Just for Swimming Pools

Have you ever stared into a cannon and wondered: "Why do cannonballs get to have all the fun?" Well, you're not alone! Back in 1870, Signor Farini (a.k.a. William Hunt from Port Hope, Ontario) came up with a human cannonball stunt, and patented a spring-loaded cannon to lauch said human through the air. Both then and now, it's important for a human cannonball to fly through the air in an arc so he or she bounces onto a net below. Needless to say, there's a lot to consider when getting from Point A (the cannon) to Point B (the net): the initial speed of the cannoneer, the angle at which the cannon was placed, the weight of the cannoneer, and whether there is any wind that can send the cannoneer off course. And when rocketing at speeds of up to 115 kilometres (70 miles) per hour, a cannoneer really doesn't want to miss Point B.

Targeting for Tacos

In 1986, the Russian space station Mir was launched into orbit around Earth. It circled our planet more than 86,000 times and was visited by over 100 astronauts. But by 2001, too many technical problems forced Mir to be brought back home. That's when Taco Bell® got in on the action. The restaurant chain floated a vinyl target on the ocean near Australia, close to where Mir was scheduled to crash. Their promise: if the space station hit the target, every American would get a free taco. The world held its breath, and Americans licked their lips in anticipation. On March 23, 2001, the space station crashed and sunk. Sadly, the target was not hit, and there were no tacos for the taking.

Barf-Bag Bonanza!

Speaking of flying, how could we forget the good old "air-sick bag," offered up on any flight. These bags aren't just in high demand when nausea hits. They're also highly prized amongst collectors of these things. It's a fairly small collecting community, but sickbaggers do swap and trade barf bags. One of the most impressive collections of airline sick bags is owned by Niek Vermeulen. He started collecting in 1979 after he used a barf bag to jot down some notes during a flight. He kept the bag, and has since amassed a collection of over 3,500 others from around 800 different airlines.

49

Peculiar Performers

Everyone loves a good show. Sure it's great to see the latest Broadway musical or your favorite musician on stage but sometimes it's the weird attractions that are the most memorable. Choose your favorite peculiar performer!

Flea Ring Circus

The golden age of the flea circus was the 1830s, thanks to master showman L. Bertolotto. His exhibitions featured flea orchestras "playing" music, fleas "dancing" in extravagant costumes, and stunts like fleas "racing" miniature chariots. Many flea circuses did not feature actual fleas at all, but instead used mechanized parts to make it look as if tiny insects were pulling toy chariots and performing other stunts. Some flea circuses did use live fleas. The showman would insist that the fleas were trained, for example, to play soccer. In reality, a chemical that fleas did not like was applied to a small ball, and it would appear as if the fleas were playing soccer because they'd kick the ball away. So you could say that a flea's kick was all trick!

MICROBE TRACK-AND-FIELD STADIUM

FINISH START

Flea circus, schmea circus . . . it's time for the
Microbe Olympics!

Did you know that microscopic organisms like bacteria live on the sweaty palms of your hands? Did you know that they are all world-class athletes?

Now, THRILL to the sight of microscopic organisms racing around this track. All you need to do is place the palm of your hand onto the track-and-field stadium. Remove your hand, then lean in close and watch those microscopic organisms RACE to the finish line!

Okay, okay, so the microbes aren't trained athletes. And they don't exactly "race" to the finish line. They do divide and multiply, though. And for the curious, the microbes you might transfer from your hand to this page could be one of the following organisms: *Staphylococcus epidermidis*, *Staphylococcus aureus*, and Corynebacteria—all different kinds of bacteria.

By the way, since they're microscopic organisms, they're really small. Smaller than this print, even. You can't actually see them with your naked eye.

Here Comes the Comet!

When British Columbia native Tom Comet injured himself snowboarding, he took up juggling on the road to recovery. Soon the new hobby became a passion, and Tom continued to juggle up to eight hours a day. Today, Tom juggles an amazing and dangerous array of items, including three flaming blowtorches. He's the world champ when it comes to juggling chainsaws, which he practices for one hour each day. In August 2002, Tom tossed three revved-up chainsaws around for 44 throws. And as the director of Circus Orange, Tom's act also sees him balancing a running lawnmower on his head. During this performance, audience members are invited to throw lettuce heads at the rotating blades. Perhaps one day he'll make the change to cabbage, allowing Tom to create the most death-defying coleslaw on the planet.

Fun with Flatulence

Although it's often embarrassing, gaseous acts of flatulence can draw quite a crowd. While doing yoga at the age of 15, an English performer known as Mr. Methane discovered he was able to "breathe out of both ends." His classmates were impressed, but Mr. Methane didn't embark on a career in flatulence until later in life, when he "opened" for a friend's band. His act was a hit, and Methane soon became a featured artist in his own right. Sporting a green mask, tights, and cape, Mr. Methane's show sees him "singing" from both ends of his body. His controlled breaking-of-wind also allows him to blow out birthday candles and fire darts at balloons.

Astounding
Abilities!

Every person on Earth is a unique individual with special talents and abilities. Some deserve special mention in a book like this one!

How to Get Ahead in Balancing

While working as a bricklayer in his native England, John Evans discovered that he had a knack for balancing bricks on a wooden board with his head. He could carry up to 24 while climbing ladders on the job. He added more, and soon he was carrying 36 bricks. That's only the beginning of this heavy-weight champ's story. Evans has become a master at balancing heavy things on his head: bikes, cement mixers, speedboats, and even Mini cars. Perhaps his ultimate act was balancing 92 people, with a total weight of 5,180 kilograms (11,420 pounds), on his head in one hour! Evans hasn't let success go to his head: by raising heavy objects, he raises money for charity.

I did a little research and found out that the weight of 92 people is the same as:

1 African Elephant
17 Siberian Tigers
760 Whooping Cranes
52,206 Goliath Beetles

Student

There's No Business Like Bee Business!

Dr. Norman Gary, a retired bee research scientist, trained 109 honeybees to fly into his mouth, closed his lips, and held them captive for a full ten seconds! He's also allowed 200,000 bees to cluster over his body. Such close company with bees has caused him to be stung more than 75,000 times during his 55 years with these insects! And just so you know, he didn't get stung when he lured the 109 bees into his mouth.

The Rattlesnake Man

No honeybees for Jackie Bibby. Since 1969, this Texas native has been handling venomous reptiles—rattlesnakes! Not only has Jackie managed to place ten rattlesnakes into a sack in 17.11 seconds, but he also is the world champ at sitting in a bathtub with rattlesnakes—81 to be exact. He's also crawled into a sleeping bag to cuddle up with 109 of these critters. In 2001, he held eight live rattlesnakes in his mouth. (Don't worry: Bibby's mouth was clamped onto their rattling ends.) Two years later, he beat his own record and shoved nine live rattlers into his mouth. In his many years of handling snakes, Bibby has been seriously bitten six times. Hope it stays that way!

What if...

...rattlesnake baths were the latest spa treatment?

Skiing Squirrel

These pages have focused on humans with spectacular skills, but what of the rest of the animal kingdom? Look no further than Twiggy, a gray squirrel hailing from Florida, who is a water-skiing wonder. Raised and taught by Lou Ann Best, Twiggy is pulled by a radio-controlled boat that jets through the waters of a pool at 8 to 10 kilometres (5 to 6 miles) per hour. The squirrel has performed at international boat shows and made appearances on all sorts of TV programs. To date, there have been five "Twiggy" squirrels that have been taught how to water-ski by Lou Ann and her late husband, Chuck. The first was found after a hurricane in the 1970s. The Bests have also taught other animals how to water-ski, including a French poodle, an armadillo, a toad, and a miniature horse.

Weird *Science*

Science is the study of how the universe operates, based on laws, experiments, and a lot of educated guesses about the nature of things. But sometimes our greatest achievements happen by accident; other times, learned people will spend endless hours working on experiments that some might consider a little bit strange.

And the Winner Is...

If you're looking to break into exciting new worlds of science where few have experimented before, you could be a contender for an Ig Nobel Prize. Since 1991, these prizes have been awarded to people whose achievements in science first make people laugh, and then make them think. In an annual celebration held at Harvard University, the "Igs" are presented by actual Nobel Prize winners, some of whom later perform fun ballet and opera pieces for the crowd. What kind of achievements do the Ig Nobel Prizes recognize? A glance at some past winners will give you a hint. They include a man from the Institute of Food Research in England for his analysis of soggy breakfast cereal, and the creator of the plastic pink flamingo.

A Real Earful

Imagine the headline: Veterinarian Turns Himself into a Human Guinea Pig. It's a true story! This vet used himself in an experiment to see if ear mites (tiny, spider-like creatures) living in cats' ears could be transmitted to people. He wiped a cotton swab in a mite-infested cat's ear, then transferred the sample to his own left ear. Almost immediately, he heard scratching and moving sounds as the mites inched their way through his ear canal. For weeks, the vet documented the sounds and activity of the mites (which he could feel crawling across his face), until finally the activity stopped. This was a relief, as the mites were quite painful. But as a dutiful scientist, he ran the experiment again on himself.

Birds + Art = Science!

The pigeons we see on our sidewalks certainly like the breadcrumbs we throw to them, but they may also have an eye for art as well. A professor at Keio University in Japan separated some pigeons into two groups. Both groups of pigeons were placed into boxes and shown paintings by famous artists Claude Monet and Pablo Picasso. To be given tasty seeds as a reward, one group had to identify paintings by Monet by pecking on a key. The other group had to peck for Picasso. Soon enough, both groups were able to correctly identify the work of each painter around 90% of the time! The pigeons were later able to tell the difference between paintings done by different artists but in similar styles. But the fun doesn't stop there! Pigeons have also been shown to tell the difference in pieces of music by classical composers. To date, no pigeons have given up their day jobs eating breadcrumbs to work as art critics.

The Echo Quacks Back

There's a long-held belief that a duck's quack doesn't produce an echo. This belief went unchallenged for a long time, until Trevor Cox of Salford University, a specialist in improving the acoustics in concert halls and movie theaters, examined the matter with the latest sound technology. Cox used computer software that would allow him to simulate a number of different sound environments, and enlisted the aid of a duck named Daisy. He recorded her quacks in a special soundproof room that had no echoes. Then Daisy was put in a larger room that enhanced echoes and was encouraged to make some noise. Although it wasn't loud, the tests proved that a duck's quack does indeed echo. Cox concluded that the "ack" part of a duck's quack blocks out the sound of the faint echo.

[...and Weirder Science]

Monkey Business

It was once theorized that in an infinite amount of time, an infinite number of monkeys randomly hitting typewriter keys would eventually produce the works of William Shakespeare. Researchers tested the theory out in the summer of 2002, by installing a computer inside the zoo enclosure of six Sulawesi crested macaques. To begin with, the monkeys showed clear signs of writer's block: the lead male hit the computer with a stone. Later the monkeys used the computer as a toilet. Eventually, the monkeys became interested in typing, particularly the letter "s"—they would write five pages consisting almost entirely of that letter. As the experiment neared its conclusion, the macaques had added the letters "a," "q," "j," "l," and "m."

Professor

Student

Hey, teach, these macaques could write "jam," "lam," and even "slam" using the letters they typed.

That seems a long way from the complete works of Shakespeare.

Never rush a monkey. Great works of literature take time.

The Perfect Cheese Sandwich

Science has been used to explain the force of gravity, the theory of relativity, and now the ultimate cheese sandwich. For his experiment, Dr. Len Fisher, a physicist from the University of Bristol in England, prepared little cheese sandwiches, then had people eat the sandwiches. He tested their breath using a device built to measure smells to determine the tastiest cheese sandwich. This isn't the first time that Fisher has taken a scientific approach to food. In 1999, he determined the best way to dunk a cookie into a mug of tea.

The Science of Shower Curtains

You step into the shower, turn on the water, and before you know it, the curtain has billowed in and clung to your wet body. Why? To answer this age-old question, a researcher at the University of Massachusetts programmed in a computer model of his shower, then turned on the water for 30 seconds. Using a sophisticated program that made 1.5 trillion calculations over two weeks, the researcher concluded that there are two reasons. First, warm air wants to rise up, and cold air from outside tries to push its way into the shower. The second force at work is the spray and the air motion inside the shower. The air inside the shower moves like a hurricane, sucking the curtain in. Twister!

When Scientists Get Irritated!

Imagine being a paleontologist (a scientist who studies prehistoric life) when a skull of a new kind of dinosaur arrives from a dig in Brazil. It's an exciting find! But the delight ended for paleontologists who realized that their "newly discovered dino" had been doctored. The people who dug it up apparently had added plaster and bits of bone to the skull to make it more awe-inspiring. The paleontologists found this out when they scanned the skull with a CAT scan for a closer inspection. They were so irritated by the "repair" job to the skull that they named this dinosaur *Irritator challengeri* (the "Irritator").

Whoops...
It's Science!

PICTURE THIS: YOU KNOCK OVER YOUR GLASS OF CRANBERRY JUICE ON THE WHITE TABLECLOTH WHILE REACHING FOR SECONDS. BEFORE YOUR PARENTS CAN GET MAD AT YOU, IT MIGHT BE A GOOD IDEA TO POINT OUT THAT GREAT ACHIEVEMENTS HAVE HAPPENED BECAUSE OF ACCIDENTS. HERE'S THE PROOF.

2. Knocking a Glass Over

In 1903, a scientist named Edouard Benedictus was working with a glass flask full of chemicals. The chemicals had evaporated, leaving a thin film on the inner surface of the glass. These chemicals would have gone unnoticed by science, but Benedictus KNOCKED OVER THE GLASS, causing it to fall to the floor of his lab. Instead of shattering into little bits, the chemicals on the flask held the glass together. Benedictus's discovery paved the way for shatterproof safety glass. Hooray for accidents!

1. Dropping a Boatload of Rubber Duckies

A shipping freighter was traveling in the Pacific Ocean when a container full of yellow rubber duckies FELL OVERBOARD into the ocean. It was a setback for people in need of bath toys, but a boon to science. An oceanographer (a scientist who studies oceans) decided to track the duckies. By following their paths and tracking where they ended up, he gathered new information about ocean currents and wind patterns.

58

3. Dropping Stuff on the Stove

In 1839, Charles Goodyear was experimenting with rubber in his kitchen, and mixed rubber with chemicals like magnesium, turpentine, alcohol, nitric acid, and sulfur. His concoction would have been a waste, but then he DROPPED THE CHEMICALS ONTO HIS STOVE. The heat from the stove "vulcanized" the rubber, which made it less brittle than ordinary rubber, and more resistant to the cold...paving the way for a rubber revolution.

4. Leaving Things by an Open Window

In 1928, Alexander Fleming was working in his laboratory with some staphylococci bacteria. He accidentally LEFT A SAMPLE BESIDE AN OPEN WINDOW and left the lab. When he returned, he found that mold had blown in and contaminated his sample. But upon further examination, he discovered that the mold had killed the bacteria. Because of this important blunder, Fleming paved the way for the discovery of penicillin, an antibiotic that has saved many lives around the world.

Student

TOP FIVE THINGS *NOT* TO LEAVE BESIDE OPEN WINDOWS

5. Blueberry pies
4. Bowling balls
3. Large stacks of paper
2. An open package of flour (especially on a windy day)
1. Live rattlesnakes*

* In fact, these are not good to leave beside closed windows, either.

A Sweet Taste Test

Sometimes a big discovery is right at—or on!—your fingertips. This is what happened to a pair of researchers at Johns Hopkins University in 1879. One of the researchers came home from the lab and TASTED SOMETHING SWEET ON HIS FINGERS. He decided to trek back to the lab to find the mysteriously sweet substance. He did a little laboratory taste test and sampled some of the chemicals they had kicking around. (Don't try this at home!) Lo and behold, he eventually found a chemical called saccharin, which turned out to be 300 to 500 times sweeter than sugar, and is now used as a sugar substitute.

Amusing ~~Amazing~~ Inventions

YOU'VE SEEN HOW SOME GREAT INVENTIONS ARE THE RESULT OF CARELESSNESS AND CHANCE. NOW SEE HOW SOME OF OUR SILLIEST INVENTIONS ARE THE RESULT OF STRANGE AND CREATIVE THOUGHTS, AND AN ACTIVE IMAGINATION....

The Fast and the Funny

Humans have invented some amazing vehicles, from hydrofoils to stealth aircraft to space shuttles. But few vehicles are as amusing as the ones created by Edd China and David Davenport of England's Cummfy Banana company. Take, for instance, the "Bog Standard," a motorcycle and sidecar with a twist: the driver is seated on a Victorian-style toilet and the passenger can stretch out in a bathtub. An actual licensed vehicle, this contraption can reach speeds of up to 114 kilometres (71 miles) per hour. China and Davenport have also created other wheeled wonders, including the "Casual Lofa," a sofa-on-wheels powered by the engine from a Mini car, and steered with a pizza pan. The front bumper is a coffee table, and the indicator lights are hidden in potted plants fixed to either side of the sofa. Truly an upholstered achievement, it seats a driver and two passengers, and is the fastest furniture around, reaching speeds of up to 140 kilometres (87 miles) per hour.

Nearly Useless

Created by Japanese inventor Kenji Kawakami, Chindogu, which means "weird tool," are inventions that have been dubbed as "unuseless" because they're almost—but not quite—useless. If your inventions are to be 100% Chindogu, they cannot be patented, and they can't just be a joke: the invention must serve a purpose. For example, a Chindogu baby mop is an outfit worn by a baby that doubles as a mop head so when the baby crawls around, the floor gets clean.

A Green Helmet

Check out this patented invention: the greenhouse helmet. Plants secured inside the helmet take in the carbon dioxide you breathe onto them (which they like), and in turn, the plants provide oxygen for you. The patent illustration does indicate a problem, though, because the plants mounted inside the helmet are prickly cacti. So what happens to someone wearing a greenhouse helmet full of cacti who trips and falls over? Yee-ouch!

This Blimp's for the Birds

Back in 1887, there were no airplanes. If you wanted to take to the sky, the only way to do it was to jump off a cliff (problem: you wouldn't actually fly, and you and your air-time would be short-lived). You could also do things the easy way and ride in a hot air balloon. One patented invention to aid hot air balloonists was the "Means and Apparatus for Propelling and Guiding Balloons." Sure, it sounded good, but there was a catch: the balloon was to be powered by "living motors." Living motors? The patent indicated these would be really big birds like condors, eagles, or vultures, which would be strapped into harnesses, and steered by the conductor. To stop the birds from flying, the conductor would throw nets over the birds. Creative, yes, but this was one invention that never really "flew."

The Silliest Invention Ever!

During the Second World War, engineer James Wright was working for an American appliance company, trying to develop a cheap substitute for synthetic rubber. When he combined boric acid with silicone oil, the result was a pink goop—stretchier and bouncier than regular rubber. It was fun, but not helpful for the war effort. Years later, an advertising copy writer came across a sample of Wright's creation and realized its potential in toy stores. He bought a load of it and packaged it into plastic eggs. The pink goop, Silly Putty®, was a big hit!

Professor

Did you know that this delightfully silly pink substance went on a trip to the moon with the Apollo 8 astronauts in 1968?

Leech Power

In the 1800s, a British doctor noticed that before a severe storm, freshwater leeches got agitated. He came up with the idea of using these leeches to warn of incoming storms. The doctor created a machine called the Tempest Prognosticator, consisting of twelve glass jars, each containing a leech. The leeches were hooked up to chains, and the chains to bells. The idea was that before a storm, the leeches would thrash around, causing the bells to ring and warning that wild weather was on the way. The doctor had high hopes, but in the end, like the leeches, his invention just sucked.

Far-Out Futures

WE'RE NEARING THE END OF THE BOOK (SNIFF, SNIFF). SO LET'S END OFF WITH A TRIP BACK IN TIME TO SEE SOME PREDICTIONS OF WHAT LIFE WOULD BE LIKE IN THE FUTURE.

Perilous Predictions at the World's Fair

"Under the symbol of the Unisphere, exhibits from all parts of the world will be gathered for your delight! You'll wonder at predictions of things to come..." So said the publicity material for the 1964 New York World's Fair, a huge exhibition that was a cornerstone of the Space Age 1960s. The exhibition offered a potential glimpse into the near future. In addition to a colony on the Moon, it imagined a city over 3,000 metres (10,000 feet) under the ocean, which could be reached by atomic-powered submarines, where workers could drill for minerals and oil, and vistors could relax at the underwater Hotel Atlantis. The exhibition also featured an atomic-powered jungle road builder, five stories tall and as long as three football fields. It was guessed that a contraption like this could manufacture 1.6 kilometres (1 mile) of above-ground highway each hour, for twenty-four hours a day. A laser tree cutter would work ahead of the road builder, cutting down trees and releasing chemicals to stop plants from growing. Yikes!

2001: The Year That Wasn't

Even the very learned can make mistakes. Look no further than writer Arthur C. Clarke, author of the famous book (and movie) *2001: A Space Odyssey*. In 1968, he wrote an article for *Vogue* magazine in which he shared his predictions for that fateful year. Clarke imagined that in 2001, an entire month's worth of food might weigh only 45 kilograms (100 pounds). He suggested that we might even be eating grass, treated by scientists to be nutritious and taste great! He wrote that houses would be built of light-enough material that they would be able to fly. Homes would be carried around by helicopterlike "sky cranes" that would allow people to head south for the winter in their own houses! Talk about traveling in comfort.

Professor

Readers should know that the same article in *Vogue* accurately predicted things like satellite television, cheap telephone rates, and home computers with "immediate access" to newspapers and libraries (i.e. the Internet).